A TASTE OF
BRITAIN

Roz Denny

Thomson Learning
New York

Titles in this series

A TASTE OF

Britain	Italy
China	Japan
France	Mexico
India	West Africa

Cover *Tower Bridge is a historic landmark on the Thames River in London.*

Frontispiece *Buttered scones with jam and a cup of strong tea with milk make a traditional British afternoon tea – a light meal eaten at about 4 p.m.*

First published in the
United States in 1994 by
Thomson Learning
115 Fifth Avenue
New York, NY 10003

First published in Great Britain in 1994 by
Wayland (Publishers) Ltd.

Library of Congress Cataloging-in-Publication Data
Denny, Roz.
A taste of Britain / Roz Denny.
p.   cm. —(Food around the world)
Includes bibliographical references and index.
ISBN 1-56847-184-X
1. Cookery, British—Juvenile literature.
2. Food habits—Great Britain—Juvenile literature.
3. Great Britain—Social life and customs—Juvenile literature.
[1. Cookery, British. 2. Food habits—Great Britain.
3. Great Britain—Social life and customs.]
I. Title. II. Series.
TX717.D39   1994
641.5941—dc20   94-2317

Printed in Italy

Contents

"Good, plain cooking"   4

The land and farming   7

British food through history   12

Food in Britain today   16

Mealtimes   19

Specialties and regional foods   24

British desserts   29

Food from gardens and allotments   31

A British Christmas   33

Shepherd's pie   35

Bubble and squeak   38

Welsh rarebit   40

Apple crumble   42

Strawberry and lemon whim-wham   44

Glossary   45

Books to read   47

Index   48

"Good, plain cooking"

"Good, plain cooking." That is how people in Britain like to describe their food. But many foreign visitors to Britain think British food is boring and often badly cooked. So what is the truth?

Britain is a very rich agricultural country. There is excellent grass for animals to graze on, top-quality crops grow plentifully, and farming is extremely efficient. British cooks have not felt it necessary to cook rich, elaborate dishes since they believe these foods are naturally full of flavor. British cooking is based on farmhouse dishes, such as roast meats, meat pies, cakes, jams, pickles –

Roast beef with vegetables. Excellent fresh produce, simply cooked, brings out the best in British cooking.

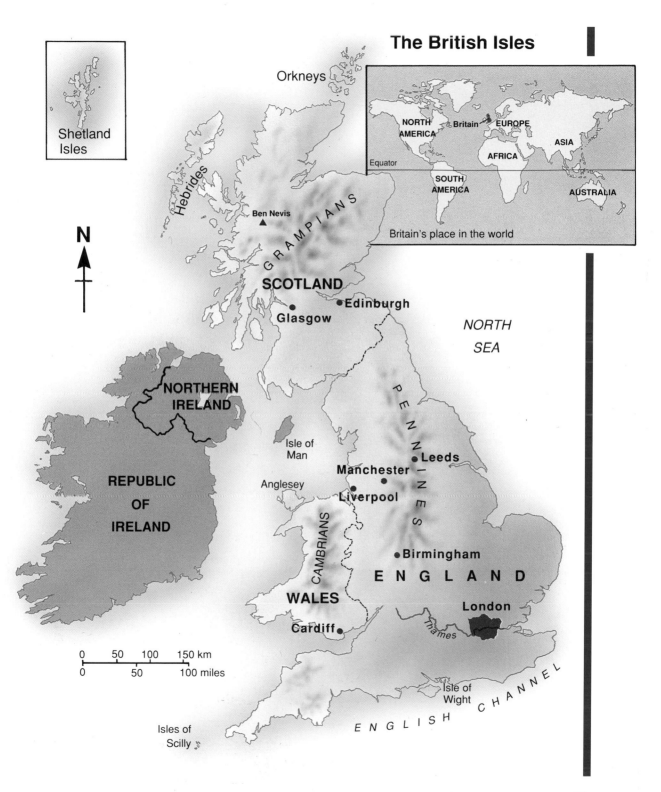

The British Isles

Orkneys

Shetland Isles

Hebrides

Ben Nevis

GRAMPIANS

SCOTLAND

Glasgow

Edinburgh

NORTH SEA

N

NORTHERN IRELAND

Isle of Man

Anglesey

REPUBLIC OF IRELAND

PENNINES

Leeds

Manchester

Liverpool

CAMBRIANS

Birmingham

WALES

ENGLAND

Cardiff

London

Thames

0   50   100   150 km
0   50   100 miles

Isle of Wight

ENGLISH CHANNEL

Isles of Scilly

NORTH AMERICA   Britain   EUROPE
ASIA
Equator   AFRICA
SOUTH AMERICA   AUSTRALIA
Britain's place in the world

and, above all, wonderful deserts. Unfortunately for many visitors to Britain, however, such good cooking may be available only in people's homes, so few tourists get to eat really good, traditional British food.

Britain is not just home to traditional, plain cooking. It was once the center of a large empire, made up of many countries and lasting from the mid-eighteenth century through to the 1950s. Many people from these other countries have come to Britain to live and work. They in turn have brought their own dishes and foods, many of which have become British favorites, especially dishes from India, Pakistan, Bangladesh, Cyprus, the West Indies, Africa, and Hong Kong. So, while we may talk about traditional British foods, in fact the normal British foods eaten today are those of a modern, multicultural society.

British society today is a mixture of people whose families have come from many parts of the world. The mix of different traditions has introduced delicious new foods to Britain.

The land and farming

Compared to many countries, Britain is very small. It is an island of less than 95,000 square miles, yet it is home to around 58 million people. Britain is the main island of the British Isles, the other being Ireland, to the west. It is situated off the west coast of northern Europe and is separated from Europe by a shallow sea, called the North Sea.

Britain actually consists of three countries – England, Scotland, and Wales. England is the biggest. Scotland lies to the north and Wales to the west. The Welsh and Scottish peoples are very proud of their "differentness," and any foreign visitor mistaking them for English will be quickly corrected.

The British capital is London. One of the biggest cities in the world, it has a population of over 6 million people. Other important cities include Leeds, Birmingham, Manchester, and Liverpool in England; Cardiff in Wales; and Glasgow and Edinburgh in Scotland.

Edinburgh, the capital of Scotland, is an ancient city with many old buildings.

A taste of Britain

Above *Purple, flowering heather on a Yorkshire moor.* Below *Ben Nevis reaches 4,406 feet above sea level.*

The countryside and climate

Britain is a mixture of different landscapes. There are gently rolling hills; wide, flat plains; wild, craggy moors; and mountain ranges that, although quite low compared to elsewhere in the world, are nevertheless quite impressive.

The main mountain ranges are the Pennines (known as the backbone of England because they run up the center of the country); the Cambrians in Wales; and the Grampians in Scotland, containing Britain's highest mountain, Ben Nevis. The most famous river is the Thames, which runs through London.

The climate is described as temperate – that is, it is neither too hot nor too cold. The rainfall is generally high, and there are few droughts. Foreign visitors (and the British themselves) often complain that it rains too much, especially in the summer.

Farming

In Britain the land is fertile and the rainfall good. This means that crops grow well and there is good grazing land for cattle and sheep. The land is easy to farm because it is not too rough and stony, and there are many excellent roads for taking produce to markets and stores. British farmers are among the most efficient in the world, and use a lot of modern machinery. As more machines are used, fewer and fewer people are needed to work on the land.

Combine harvesters are used to cut cereal crops.

A taste of Britain

Fruit farms produce apples for eating or making into juice or cider.

In general, the south and east of Britain produce cereals and fodder crops including wheat, corn, and rapeseed. In cooler parts of Britain, particularly Scotland, oats and barley are grown. Barley is used to make Scotch, or Scottish whisky. Across southern England there are fruit farms where apples (for eating or making into cider), strawberries, raspberries, and cherries are grown. In the southwest, where the grass is rich, cattle are raised for dairy products and beef. This area is famous for its thick cream and cheeses.

In southwest England, where the rainfall is high, the lush, green grass is ideal for grazing dairy cattle.

In hilly areas, such as those in north Wales and Scotland, the land cannot be plowed for cereal crops. Here, sheep are raised, for both their wool and their meat.

Fishing used to be an important industry all around the coast of Britain. Herring, mackerel, salmon, haddock, and cod were caught and preserved by salting or smoking. This led to specialities such as kippers (smoked herring) and smoked salmon. Today, most fishing is carried out off the coasts of eastern Scotland and northeast England.

Sheep are raised on the mountains of Snowdonia, in Wales.

Fishing boats in harbor on the east coast of Scotland.

British food through history

Many traditional British dishes still eaten today have developed from recipes used long ago. These dishes often have unusual, amusing names, whose original meaning is now difficult for us to understand. For example: "maids of honor" are little sweet tarts; "singing hinnies" are flat, fruity scones, cooked on a griddle, which seem to sing as they sizzle; "toad-in-the-hole" consists of sausages cooked in batter in the oven.

"Toad-in-the-hole" and (below) *a picture of a pineapple dating from the early 1600s.*

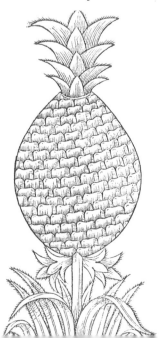

During the sixteenth century, many British sailors set off to explore North and South America (not long before this, no one in Europe had known that the Americas existed). From the reign of Queen Elizabeth I (1558-1603) on, new foods from America, such as tomatoes, potatoes, and pineapples, were brought to Britain and grown by farmers in fields and hothouses. Potatoes were to become an essential part of British cooking.

During the late eighteenth century, British farmers invented many new farming methods and machines. British farming became very efficient.

As a result, food was plentiful. Animals could be fed through the winter on fodder crops instead of being killed in the autumn. Fresh milk, cheese, butter, and meat became available throughout the winter.

Up until the nineteenth century, many foreign travelers to Britain thought the food served in inns and homes was some of the best in Europe. However, by the reign of Queen Victoria (1837-1901) Britain had become an industrial country. People were encouraged to work hard and make a lot of money.

Jethro Tull was a famous British inventor in the eighteenth century. This is a diagram of his machine for planting seeds.

A taste of Britain

In Victorian times, children from well-off families ate in their nursery, away from adults.

These hard-working Victorians believed that plainly cooked food and good table manners were more important than how the food tasted. The image of poor British food probably dates from this time.

Food in a Tudor kitchen

As an example of British food in the past, we can discover what was eaten by Tudor kings and queens, such as Henry VIII and Elizabeth I, over 400 years ago. Surprisingly, many Tudor dishes would be familiar to British people today. There were huge sides of roast beef and roast pork, delicious pies and puddings, fruits, ale (a sort of beer), rich cheeses, butter, and cream. Fresh vegetables, unusual salad plants, and herbs were grown in the gardens of both rich and poor people. Plants included purslane, corn salad, sorrel, chives, sage, and mint.

The royal kitchens were huge and open. Large roasts of meat were cooked in front of a roaring fire and turned on a revolving spit by small kitchen boys.

Bread was the staple food for most people. There was a rough brown bread for the poor and better-quality white bread for the wealthy. Much bread was eaten. In fact, thick slices of bread were used as plates, called trenchers. Leftover bread was always used up and was often made into stuffing for roast meats.

A royal feast in 1491. The noblewoman is eating from a trencher of bread.

Food in Britain today

A stallholder in London selling yams and plantains – traditional ingredients of Caribbean cooking.

British people today enjoy many dishes and recipes from all over the world. Pasta from Italy, American-style hamburgers, and stir-fry dishes from the Far East are now all thought to be normal everyday food.

In particular, dishes from Asia and the Caribbean have become very popular. Britain has had links with these places since the days of its empire. In the 1950s and 1960s many people from the Caribbean, India, and Pakistan came to live and work in Britain, bringing their own styles of cooking with them. Indian-style curries, for example, are now eaten in many homes, as well as traditional

A family enjoying traditional Asian snack food.

British dishes such as shepherd's pie and fish and chips (french fries). In fact British people sometimes mix the two types of food – curry and chips, for example.

Another trend in British eating is vegetarianism. Many people in Britain are now becoming vegetarians, particularly young people. Supermarkets now sell more and more foods that are free of animal products, and schools offer vegetarian choices at lunchtime.

This graph shows how the number of vegetarians in Britain has increased in recent years. The number of people who do not eat red meat (beef and lamb, for example) has grown even more quickly. (Source: The Vegetarian Society.)

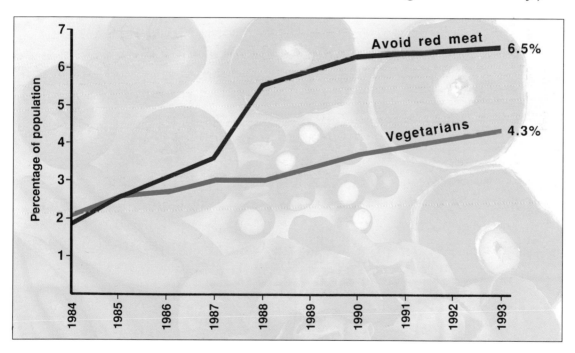

Shopping
Traditionally, food is bought from individual shops – butchers, greengrocers, fishmongers, and bakers. Some towns have markets selling fresh produce, often homegrown.

Today, however, more and more food shopping is done in large supermarkets built on the edges of town. Many dishes are sold ready-cooked, either fresh or frozen, and only need to be reheated (more than half of all British homes have a microwave oven, which can be used for reheating food). In many British families both parents go to work, and ready-cooked meals are quick and easy.

Many pubs are hundreds of years old. They always have a name. This one is called the "Rose and Crown."

Fish and chips from the fish-and-chip shop – a famous British tradition.

Eating out

No British town or village is complete without at least one public house (or pub, for short). These are inns serving drinks such as beer, wine, and spirits. Pubs provide a warm, relaxed atmosphere where people can meet and chat. Many serve cheap "pub grub," especially at lunch time. Typical food might be sandwiches, meat pies, or a "plowman's lunch" (see page 28).

In addition, there are a great many restaurants. Usually, these specialize in dishes from a foreign country – for example from India, Thailand, Italy, or the United States.

British people often like to buy hot, ready-cooked food from shops called "takeaways." These do a brisk trade in chips, so they are sometimes nicknamed "chippies." The most traditional are fish-and-chip shops, selling fresh fish that has been dipped in batter and fried until crisp, served with thick-cut chips.

Mealtimes

Mealtimes in Britain can cause some confusion – even among the British! The type of meal, the time, and what it is called all vary in different parts of the country. Even more confusingly, the same word can be used to describe very different meals.

The main meal is generally called dinner, and this can be in the early evening or in the middle of the day (the midday meal may also be called lunch). Typical main meals are grilled meat, chops, sausages, fried fish, or a stew.

A typical main meal that might be eaten at home, at a café, or in a cafeteria: fish with potatoes and peas, served with bread and butter and a cup of tea.

An example of high tea in Scotland: bread and butter, cold meat, salad, scones, pie, and fruit cake.

School dinner usually consists of a hot main course of meat or fish, with potatoes and vegetables, followed by dessert.

These will usually be served with potatoes and other vegetables.

In the industrial north, where many people traditionally worked in factories or mines, the main meal is served at about 6 p.m. That is when the workers would return home tired and hungry after work. In some parts of Britain this main meal is called high tea, or simply tea. There is meat, fish or pot-pie, with vegetables and bread and butter, followed by pudding or cake. To drink there is tea or beer. Then, before bedtime there is another, light meal, called supper. This is eaten at about 10 p.m. and may consist of cheese and biscuits (crackers), fruit cake, or even a quick meal from the local takeout.

In other parts of Britain, mostly in the south, the main meal is at lunchtime, at around 1 p.m. However, this is becoming less popular as more people work some distance from home. Many people now eat a quick sandwich or other snack in the middle of the day and have a hot main meal at about 7 p.m. Many people call *this* main evening meal supper.

School meals

Most British schoolchildren eat lunch at school in the middle of the day. This may be a hot meal provided by the school, or children may bring their own lunches, each called a "packed lunch," consisting of a sandwich, crisps (potato

chips), fruit, and a drink. The hot meals are called school dinners and usually offer a choice of meat, fish, or salad meals, plus a dessert or fruit.

Many schoolchildren take a packed lunch to school.

A full English fried breakfast.

Breakfast

As in many other parts of the world, British people mostly eat a light breakfast of cereal, toast and marmalade, and tea or coffee. Traditionally, however, Britain is famous for magnificent and large cooked breakfasts. Nowadays, people may eat a cooked breakfast only on weekends. The meal will start with fresh grapefruit or fruit juice, followed by a plate of fried food such as bacon, sausages, egg, tomato, black pudding (see page 26), and a crisp, golden slice of fried bread.

A taste of Britain

In Scotland (and elsewhere in Britain when the weather is cold), porridge (oatmeal) is popular at breakfast time. It is a thick mixture of oats, milk, and water and is a warm way to start the day.

Sunday lunch

Sunday lunch is usually served at midday and is a popular time for family and friends to get together and enjoy a large meal. The main course will be a roast, such as beef, lamb, pork, or chicken, served with roast potatoes, boiled vegetables, and gravy (a light sauce made with the juices from the meat). In many parts of Britain, roast beef is accompanied by little crisp puffs of batter, called Yorkshire puddings. The main course is followed by a sweet dessert, such as apple pie or trifle.

This family is enjoying Sunday lunch of roast beef and Yorkshire pudding.

Afternoon tea

This a very British meal. It is thought to have been started as a fashion by the Duchess of Bedford in 1840. The Duchess got hungry between lunch, served at midday, and dinner in the evening, so she had tea at about 4 p.m. The main part of the meal is a pot of freshly brewed tea, served with milk and sugar or slices of lemon. Then there are plates of thin sliced bread and butter; sandwiches of cucumber, egg, or tomato; buttered scones with jam; and pieces of sponge cake or fruit cake.

Traditional afternoon tea can be rather dainty. This one consists of small, neat sandwiches, scones with thick cream and jam, cake – and of course tea.

Specialties and regional foods

Pies and pastries

Cold meat pies are made with pork, ham, or veal wrapped in a crisp, rich pastry called hot watercrust pastry. The meat is chopped fine and put inside the pastry raw. When cooked and cooled, the meat is solid and the pie easy to cut into slices. These pies are popular for picnics and packed lunches.

Pork pie is cut into thick slices.

There are also hot meat pies, the most famous of which is steak and kidney pie. Chunks of beef and kidney are stewed in a gravy, then put into a pie dish, topped with pastry, and baked.

Other pastries are called pasties. The most famous are from Cornwall, in the southwest, and are called Cornish pasties. These individual pies are half-moon-shaped envelopes of pastry, filled with ground beef, potato, and onion. In the past, pasties were a good way for people to take a large snack to work with them, to eat in the middle of the day. In the town of Luton people ate a pasty that contained meat at one end and apple at the other. In this way, they could eat a meat course and dessert in one handful.

A crisp, rich pastry, called shortcrust, is used to make Cornish pasties.

Stews

Stews and casseroles are dishes of meat, such as beef, pork, or chicken, plus lots of vegetables, cooked slowly in stock or gravy in the oven until the meat is tender. Lancashire hot pot is a popular dish from the north of England. This is a stew topped with slices of potato that turn golden and crisp when baked in the oven.

In the past, to make a little meat stretch to feed large, hungry families, cooks would make little dumplings of flour and suet. These would be placed on top of the bubbling stew for the last half-hour of cooking.

Lancashire hot pot is a meat stew topped with slices of potato.

A taste of Britain

British "bangers" are usually small and fat and served hot.

A Scottish butcher selling haggis.

Sausages

Sausages in Britain are quite different from those in the rest of Europe. They are made of fresh meat, usually ground pork, mixed with breadcrumbs and spices. There are many different types from different regions. Sausages are popular in Britain, where they are called "bangers." They are either fried or grilled. Sausages can be served for breakfast with eggs, bacon, and tomatoes, or as a main meal with mashed potatoes or french fries and vegetables.

Other sausages are made with offal. One of these is called black pudding, eaten mostly in the north of England. It is a sausage made of pig's blood mixed with breadcrumbs and spices.

A specialty from Scotland is called haggis. This is a mixture of offal, oatmeal, onion, and spices, stuffed into a sheep's stomach. It is boiled and usually served with mashed turnips.

Cheeses

Most of Britain's cheeses are hard and made from cow's milk. Many have been made the same way for hundreds of years.

There are nine main types of British cheese. Most have regional names, such as Red Leicester, Caerphilly, Cheshire, Stilton, and so on, but they can also be made in other counties. One of them, Cheddar, is perhaps the most imitated cheese in the world, with versions made

British cheeses are usually made in large cylinder shapes, called truckles, from which triangular wedges are cut.

in other countries such as New Zealand, Australia, Ireland, and the United States.

Bread

If it is well made by local bakers, British bread can be among the best in the world – light, crusty, and full of flavor. Unfortunately, much of the bread sold in Britain is mass-produced and is sold presliced in plastic bags.

In recent years, however, supermarkets and stores have been selling breads made according to old recipes.

British bakers also sell simple but delicious buns and cakes. Hot cross buns, marked with a cross, are eaten at Easter; scones are plain buns, split open and buttered; Eccles cakes are round parcels of pastry filled with dried fruit.

A plowman's lunch

A plowman's lunch is a light meal often served in pubs. It is basically bread, cheese, and pickles. It is very easy to do yourself.

Cut some British cheeses, such as Cheddar, Stilton, Cheshire, or Red Leicester, into wedges. Allow about 4 ounces of cheese per person. Lay it on a plate with chunks of crusty bread, some pickled onions, chutney, a fresh tomato, and some lettuce.

British desserts

The British generally call the dessert course "pudding." Some of the best British recipes are for desserts. Many have wonderful, funny names such as trifle, brown betty, spotted dick, fool, crumble, roly-poly, and so on. Desserts are often served with custard, a thick sauce of milk, eggs, and sugar, flavored with vanilla.

Here is a list of popular "puddings."
Trifle This is a cold pudding consisting of pieces of cake soaked in sherry or fruit juice, layered with fresh fruit, sometimes topped with jelly, and the whole covered with whipped cream.
Fool Another cold pudding, made by mixing whipped cream with custard and adding stewed fruit such as gooseberries or rhubarb.
Crumble A hot pudding with a fruit base, such as chopped apples, blackberries, or gooseberries, topped with a crumbly mixture of flour, butter, and sugar.
Roly-poly This hot pudding consists of a strip of suet pastry, spread with jam or

Rhubarb fool is a smooth mixture of cream, custard, and stewed fruit.

A taste of Britain

Summer pudding is made by lining a pudding bowl with bread and filling it with lightly cooked juicy fruits (or fruits that have been sugared to create juice), such as raspberries and red currants. The pudding is left to chill in the refrigerator until the juice has soaked through the bread. It can then be turned out onto a plate.

Treacle tart is sweet and sticky.

fruit and rolled up like a jellyroll. It is then baked in the oven.

Syllabub This is one of Britain's oldest puddings. In Tudor times it was made of wine mixed with fresh milk flavored with sugar and spices. King Charles II, who ruled from 1660 to 1685, is said to have milked cows in St. James's Park, London, straight into his glass of red wine. Nowadays, syllabub is made by mixing whipped cream with sugar, lemon, and, sometimes, sherry.

Dessert pancakes Light, hot, thin rounds of fried batter, made from eggs, flour, and milk. In Britain, Shrove Tuesday is also called Pancake Day. This is the day before Lent, which is a period of fasting for Christians. The idea was that you used up foods such as eggs and flour before starting to fast. On Pancake Day, people have fun cooking pancakes, tossing them into the air and catching them in the pan to cook both sides.

Treacle tart This is a pastry tart base filled with golden syrup (which used to be called treacle), breadcrumbs, grated lemon rind, and ground ginger.

Food from gardens and allotments

The British enjoy gardening. Many people like to grow their own fresh vegetables and fruits, such as potatoes, green beans, apples, and raspberries. In towns, where houses may have small yards, gardeners can pay to use a small plot of land, called an allotment, owned by the local town council.

Above *Allotments are used for growing vegetables.*
Below *A day out at a pick-your-own farm.*

Nowadays, many fruit farmers grow soft fruits, such as strawberries, and allow people to pick the fruit for themselves. These are called "pick-your-own" farms, and they are very popular.

With so much fresh produce in the summer months, the British have developed ways of preserving fruit and vegetables to last through the winter. There are all kinds of delicious jams, jellies, pickles, and chutneys.

Jams and jellies
Jams are made by boiling fruit with sugar until they set (become firm, not

runny). Jellies are made in the same way, but only the juice of the fruit is used. Popular jams are made of strawberries, raspberries, and plums. One of the most popular fruit preserves is marmalade. This is a chunky, bittersweet orange jam that it is eaten on toast for breakfast.

Jams are spread on toast and scones (see photograph on title page) and used to sandwich layers of sponge cake together. They are also spooned into small pastry tarts. Jellies are often eaten with meat – red currant jelly with lamb, for example.

Fruit curds, such as lemon curd, are another way of preserving fruit. Curds are like thick custards and are made of fruit pulp or juice, cooked with eggs, butter, and sugar until thickened.

Pickles and chutneys

A jar of pickled onions.

Pickles are prepared vegetables, such as baby onions, cucumbers, and cauliflower, preserved in vinegar and spices. After pickling, the vegetables have a strong, tangy flavor. They are served with cold meats and cheeses.

Chutneys came from India and were introduced in Britain in the nineteenth century. They are mixtures of chopped fruits and vegetables, such as apples, mangoes, tomatoes, and onions, cooked with sugar, vinegar, and spices.

A British Christmas

The Christian festival of Christmas, which celebrates the birth of Jesus Christ, is the main public holiday in Britain. Many offices and factories close for up to two weeks, from the afternoon of Christmas Eve (December 24) until after New Year's Day (January 1). The days before Christmas are a time for parties and going out with friends. On Christmas Day itself (December 25) families get together to exchange presents – and eat!

The traditional Christmas still celebrated today started in Victorian times in the nineteenth century. The main meal is eaten in the middle of the day or early evening. After much preparation in the kitchen, the family sits down together to eat. The table is laid with candles and holly and each person is given a cracker (a party favor) to pull.

The centerpiece of the meal is roast turkey. This is

For Christmas lunch, roast turkey is served with roast potatoes, vegetables, and cranberry sauce (bottom left).

A taste of Britain

Flaming brandy gives a special flavor to rich, dark Christmas pudding.

Mince pies filled with mincemeat.

served with lots of side dishes, such as roast potatoes, Brussels sprouts, chestnuts, thin sausages, bacon rolls, and stuffing made of breadcrumbs, onions, and herbs that is "stuffed" inside the turkey and cooked inside it. For sauces, there is cranberry sauce, a creamy white sauce called bread sauce, and gravy.

For dessert there is a magnificent, hot, steamed pudding, called Christmas pudding. This is made to a very old recipe dating back hundreds of years. It consists of breadcrumbs, sugar, rich dried fruits, such as raisins and sultanas, nuts, spices, and suet. The pudding is usually made about six weeks before Christmas. Today, many people buy ready-made puddings from stores and supermarkets. The Christmas pudding is brought to the table with great ceremony – brandy is poured over it and set alight, to great cheers from the family.

Other Christmas treats are mince pies. These are small tarts filled with a dried-fruit mixture called mincemeat. In the past, this mixture really did have minced beef in it, as well as fruits, spices, and sugar. Sometimes, people also like to have a rich fruit cake, covered with marzipan and sweet white icing, to eat on Christmas afternoon.

Shepherd's pie

This is a popular mid-week meal with a meaty filling and creamy potato topping. Traditionally, the meat used was leftover lamb or beef from the Sunday roast, so this dish was often served on Mondays. Nowadays, fresh meat may be used, so it can be dished up on any day of the week.

Shepherd's pie is a warm, filling meal.

Ingredients
Serves 4

1 lb. fresh ground
    beef or lamb
2-3 tablespoons
    vegetable oil
1 onion, peeled and
    chopped
2 medium carrots,
    peeled and
    chopped
2½ cups stock (make
    this by putting a
    bouillon cube in
    boiling water)
1 teaspoon dried,
    mixed herbs
1 tablespoon
    Worcestershire
    sauce (if you like)
2 lbs. potatoes,
    peeled and halved
pat of butter or low-
    fat spread
a little milk
salt and ground black
    pepper

1 Fry the meat in the oil in one of the saucepans until browned, stirring well with the wooden spoon to break up any lumps.

2 Stir in the onion and carrot. Fry gently for 5 minutes until softened. Pour in the stock, and stir in the herbs, Worcestershire sauce (if using), salt, and pepper.

3 Bring to a boil, then turn down the heat and cook, without a lid, for about 20 minutes, stirring occasionally. Cool and pour into a casserole dish.

4 Meanwhile, boil the potatoes in another saucepan in plenty of water for about 15 minutes or until just tender. Test them by sticking in a knife – if it goes in easily the potatoes are cooked. Carefully drain off the water through a colander in the sink.

5 Return the potatoes to the pan and mash with the masher, making sure you get rid of all the lumps. Stir in the butter or spread and enough milk to make the potatoes soft but not runny. Add salt and pepper.

Always be careful in the kitchen. Hot oil and boiling liquid can burn. A hot oven can be dangerous. Ask an adult to help you.

6 Spoon the potato onto the meat and spread it over the top with the back of a fork.

7 Heat your broiler until it is very hot. Put the pie under the broiler and brown the top until golden and bubbling. Serve with freshly boiled cabbage or Brussels sprouts.

Bubble and squeak

This is a breakfast dish using up leftover
vegetables. It is thought of as a cockney
dish (cockneys are people born and
brought up in the East End of London). It
is often served with fried eggs, bacon,
and sausages. If you are vegetarian, serve
it with grilled mushrooms and tomatoes
instead. This dish really does bubble
and squeak as it cooks!

Bubble and squeak (bottom).

Always be careful when frying. Ask an adult to help you.

1 Fry the onion in the oil in a frying pan for about 5 minutes until just softened. Remove and mix into the cold, mashed potato.

2 Cut the cabbage into thin strips and mix into the potato. Add salt, pepper, and a pinch or two of nutmeg.

3 Shape the mixture into 6 little patties with your hands. It may help to wet your hands in cold water first. Place the patties on a plate. Heat up more oil in the frying pan.

4 When the oil is quite hot, carefully slip the patties into the pan using the spatula. Fry gently on each side for about 3-5 minutes until browned, golden and crisp.

5 Put on a plate covered with a paper towel. This will soak up any excess oil. Serve warm with other breakfast foods.

Welsh rarebit

Ingredients

Serves 4

5 oz. cheese (e.g.,
   Cheddar, Red
   Leicester, or
   Caerphilly)
butter
2 tablespoons milk
ground black pepper
dry mustard
4 slices bread

Equipment

grater
saucepan
tablespoon
wooden spoon
oven mitts

Welsh rarebit is an easy-to-make snack.

The word "supper" means different things in different parts of Britain. Sometimes it means a light meal before bedtime, sometimes it means a full-size meal at about 7 p.m. A popular light supper dish is Welsh rarebit.

1 Grate the cheese on the largest holes on the grater.

2 Melt 2 tablespoons of butter in a saucepan with 2 tablespoons of milk. Add the cheese, pepper, and a pinch of mustard.

3 Melt carefully until thickened, stirring with a wooden spoon. Do not let it boil. Keep the mixture warm.

Always be careful when using the oven. Wear oven mitts. Ask an adult to help you.

4 Heat your broiler and toast the bread.

5 Spread the cheese mixture on the toast. Return to the broiler and cook until lightly browned and bubbling. Serve right away. Eat with a knife and fork.

Apple crumble

Ingredients
Serves 4-6

1¼ cups white flour,
   or use half whole
   wheat flour and
   half plain white
   flour
6 tablespoons butter
   or margarine,
   chilled
about 5 tablespoons
   granulated sugar
1⅔ lbs. cooking
   apples, e.g.,
   Macintosh or
   Granny Smiths
½ teaspoon ground
   cinnamon
1 tablespoon light
   brown sugar

Equipment
large mixing bowl
apple peeler
small knife
medium pie dish
tablespoon
baking sheet
oven mitts

This is an easy-to-make hot dessert that
is delicious served with custard, cream,
yogurt, or ice cream. You could use
other fruit instead of apples, such as
pears, pineapple, or bananas. In the
autumn, try adding a handful or two of
blackberries to the apples.

*Apple crumble is a warming dessert,
particularly popular in autumn and winter.*

1 Put the flour into the mixing bowl. Cut the butter or margarine into small chunks and add to the flour.

2 Using the tips of your fingers (which should be very clean), rub the butter or margarine into the mixture, lifting your fingers up in the air and letting the flour fall down. This is known as "rubbing-in." Do this until the mixture looks like fine crumbs. Stir in half the granulated sugar.

3 Peel the apples. Using a small knife, cut them into quarters, then carefully cut out the core. Chop the fruit into small chunks.

4 Put the apple into a pie dish and sprinkle over the remaining sugar and the cinnamon. Splash about 5 tablespoons of water on top.

5 Sprinkle the crumble mixture on top, spreading it evenly over the fruit. Sprinkle on the light brown sugar. Place the pie dish on a baking sheet.

6 Preheat the oven to 375°F. Bake the crumble for about 30 minutes until the topping is golden brown and the apples are bubbling underneath. Remove from the oven using oven mitts and cool the crumble before serving.

Strawberry and lemon whim-wham

Ingredients
Serves 6

1 cup whipping cream, or ½ cup cream and ½ cup natural yogurt
grated rind of 1 large lemon
2 tablespoons sugar
6 ladyfingers
½ lb. strawberries, sliced
a few slivered or sliced almonds

Equipment

whisk
bowl
small knife and chopping board
fine grater
six glasses, e.g., wine glasses (the prettier the better)

This is a quick version of trifle. In the past, cooks would "wham" in fruit and pieces of cake according to their "whim."

1 Whip the cream with the lemon rind and sugar until fairly stiff. If you are using yogurt, whip the cream then fold in the yogurt.

2 Break up the ladyfingers and place in the base of the glasses. Scatter on the strawberries.

3 Spoon on the cream, decorate with almonds, and chill in the refrigerator.

This trifle contains custard as well as cream.

Glossary

Batter A thick liquid made of flour, egg, and milk. It is used for making pancakes and for coating food before frying.

Brandy A strong alcoholic drink.

Capital The main city of a country. The capital is usually the center of government.

Casserole A kind of stew. The word refers to the pottery or glass dish, with a lid, in which the stew is cooked.

Chips (In Britain) French fries.

Climate The kind of weather a place generally has.

Colander A big pan with holes in it for draining food.

Cracker A party favor in the form of a paper tube containing a paper hat or other toy and made so as to go off with a bang when the ends are pulled.

Crisps (In Britain) Potato chips.

Droughts Periods when there is little or no rain.

Dumplings Balls of sticky dough served with stews.

Efficient Working very well, with no wasted effort.

Empire A group of many countries all ruled under one person – the emperor.

Fasting Going without food or without certain foods.

Fertile When referring to soil, fertile means very rich and nourishing, thus encouraging plants to grow.

Fishmonger Someone who sells fish to the public.

Fodder crops Crops such as hay or corn grown especially for animal feed.

Graze To feed on the grass or other plants in a field.

Greengrocer Someone who sells fresh fruit and vegetables to the public.

Griddle A round iron hot plate used for cooking scones.

Herbs Plants with a delicious smell, used in cooking to flavor food.

Hothouse A building with a glass roof and walls in which the air can be kept very hot. It is used for growing plants, and is also called a greenhouse.

Marmalade Jam made from oranges.

Marzipan A paste made of ground almonds, sugar, and egg whites. It is often spread over cakes.

Moors Large areas of land, usually covered with coarse grass and heather.

Multicultural Including the various traditions of people from many different races and backgrounds.

Offal The internal parts of an animal that can be eaten. For example, liver and kidneys are offal.

Preserve To prepare food so that it does not go bad, for example by freezing, drying, salting, or pickling.

Rapeseed From a rape plant, these seeds give oil that is used as a lubricant. The leaves of the rape plant are used to feed sheep and hogs.

Recipe A list of ingredients and instructions for making a dish of food.

Scone A soft, flat, round muffin baked on a griddle.

Society The system of customs, traditions and organizations shared by one group of people.

Spices Flavorings, usually made from plants, with a strong taste and smell. For example, ginger and cinnamon are spices.

Spirits Strong alcoholic drinks such as brandy, whisky, or gin.

Spit A rod used for roasting meat. The meat is put on the rod, which can be turned slowly over a fire or other source of heat.

Staple Most important. A staple food is the food eaten as the main part of a person's diet, such as bread or rice.

Stock A liquid made by boiling meat or fish bones and vegetables in water.

Suet A special kind of very hard animal fat.

Traditional According to customs that have been handed down over the centuries.

Trend A general tendency.

Vanilla The pod or bean from the vanilla plant, which has a strong taste and is used to flavor food, especially sweet foods such as ice cream.

Vegetarianism A way of eating that excludes all meat and fish.

Vinegar A sour-tasting liquid made from the alcohol in beer, wine, or cider.

Whisky A strong alcoholic drink made from barley.

Worcestershire sauce A tangy, dark-brown liquid made from soybeans, vinegar, and spices. Because it is strong, very little is needed to flavor food.

Books to Read

Information books

England in Pictures.
Minneapolis: Lerner
Publications, 1990.

Haimes, George. *Wales.* New
York: Chelsea House, 1990.

Peplow, Mary and Shipley,
Debra. *England.* World in
View. Milwaukee: Raintree
Steck-Vaughn, 1990.

Sproule, Anna. *Great Britain:
The Land and Its People.*
Morristown, NJ: Silver
Burdett Press, 1991.

Stadtler, Christa. *The United
Kingdom.* Our Country. New
York: Bookwright Press,
1992.

Sutherland, Dorothy B.
Scotland. Enchantment of
the World. Chicago:
Childrens Press, 1985.

Recipe Books

*Better Homes and Gardens
New Junior Cookbook.* Des
Moines: Meredith Corp.,
1989.

Hill, Barbara. *Cooking the
English Way.* Minneapolis:
Lerner Publications, 1982.

Wilkes, Angela. *My First
Cookbook.* New York: Alfred
A. Knopf, 1989.

Acknowledgments

The publishers would like to thank the following for allowing their photographs to be reproduced: Anthony Blake Photo Library 12 top (G. Buntrock), 21 bottom, 26 top, 34 top, 44; Bridgeman Art Library 14 (Christopher Wood Gallery, London); Cephas 4, 30 both; Chapel Studios 38, 40, 42 (all Z. Mukhida); Greg Evans International *cover,* 10 bottom (G. B. Evans), 11 bottom (A. Ramsay), 28 (G. B. Evans), 33 (G. B. Evans); Mary Evans 13, 15; Eye Ubiquitous 6 (J. Okwesa), 11 top (P. Thompson), 18 top (P. Thompson), 21 top (P. Seheult), 29, 31 bottom, 35; Chris Fairclough Colour Library 22; Fotomas Index 12 bottom; Tony Stone Worldwide *frontispiece* (E. Craddock), 7 (D. Muscroft), 18 bottom (J. Calder), 19 (S. Yeo), 23 (R. Weller), 24, 27 (A. Blake), 32, 34 bottom (S. and N. Geary); Topham 16 top, 25 bottom, 26 bottom, 31 top (M. Rodgers); Simon Warner 8 both; Wayland Picture Library *cover inset* (A. Blackburn), 9, 10 top, 16 bottom (M. Power), 17, 20 top (A. Hasson), 20 bottom; Zefa 25 top.

The map artwork on page 5 and graph artwork on page 17 were supplied by Peter Bull. The recipe artwork on pages 36-37, 39, 41, 43, and 44 was supplied by Judy Stevens.

Index

Americas, the, foods from 12
Asian food 16

bread 15, 27-28
bread sauce 34
Britain
  cities 7
  cooking traditions 4, 6
  geography 7-8
  map 5
  multicultural society 6
British empire 6, 16
bubble and squeak 38-39

cakes 23, 28, 32, 34
Caribbean food 16
cattle 9, 10
cheeses 10, 26-27, 28
Christmas 33-34
chutney 31, 32
climate 8-9
Cornish pasties 25
cranberry sauce 34
crops 9, 10
custard 29

dairy products 10
desserts 22, 29-30, 34, 42-43, 44

dumplings 25
England 7, 8, 10
farming 4, 9-11
fish and chips 17, 18
fishing 11
fruit farms 10, 31

gardening 31
gravy 22, 34

history 12-15

jam 23, 31-32

Lancashire hot pot 25

marmalade 21, 32
mealtimes, 19-23
mince pie 34
mountains 8

packed lunches 20-21
pickles 28, 31, 32
pies 24-25
plowman's lunches 28
population 7
pork pies 24
porridge 22
potatoes 12
public houses 18, 28

ready-cooked meals 18
restaurants 18
roast meat 4, 22, 33, 35

sausages 21, 26
school meals 20-21
scones 23, 28, 32
Scotland 7, 8, 10, 11, 22, 26
sheep 9, 11
shepherd's pie 17, 35-37
shopping 17-18
stews 25
stuffing 15, 34
Sunday lunch 22

Thames River 8
Tudor times 12, 14-15
turkey 33

vegetarianism 17
Victorian times 13-14, 33

Wales 7, 8, 11
Welsh rarebit 40-41
Worcestershire sauce 36

Yorkshire pudding 22